PARADISE
ROAD TO HANA, MAUI

Pak So *&* Anna Tan

www.HanaInMay.com

Paradise: Road to Hana, Maui
Spectacular Hawaii Road Trips

Printed in Canada, 2006, First Edition
ISBN 0-9777855-0-5

Dedicated to romantics everywhere.

No alien land in all the world has any deep strong charm for me but that one, no other land could so longingly and so beseechingly haunt me, sleeping and waking, through half a lifetime, as that one has done. Other things leave me, but it abides; other things change, but it remains the same. For me its balmy airs are always blowing, its summer seas flashing in the sun; the pulsing of its surfbeat is in my ear; I can see its garlanded crags, its leaping cascades, its plumy palms drowsing by the shore, its remote summits floating like islands above the cloud rack; I can feel the spirit of its woodland solitudes, I can hear the plash of its brooks; in my nostrils still lives the breath of flowers that perished twenty years ago.

{ Mark Twain }

Introduction

Humans. We lead fast-paced lives in our modern world of up-to-the-minute information and ever-changing technology. As part of our daily reality, we are confronted by aggressive personalities, flashing electronic signs, and indescribable noises blaring from our mainland cities. Most people yearn to get off the beaten path for a little while and return to a simpler place and time.

Seeking an Eden that they hope still exists, over six million visitors escape to the Hawaiian Islands each year. The travelers arrive with visions of an endless summer, picture-perfect beaches, and spectacular scenery dancing through their heads. Having practiced a hundred years' worth of hospitality in the tourism industry, the Hawaiian Islands of Maui, Kaua'i, O'ahu, Moloka'i, Lana'i, and the Big Island meet and exceed all expectations. If you happen to "talk story" with the local residents (kama'aina) though, ask them where they go to find their Shangri-La. Where do they seek peace and perfection? You will inevitably be pointed in the direction of Hana, Maui – The Last Hawaiian Place.

It is no coincidence that Maui has been voted "Best Island in the World" for well over a decade by the readers of Condé Nast Traveler magazine. Measuring 728 square miles, Maui is named after the demigod in Hawaiian legends who used his fishhook to physically pull this chain of islands out of the sea. The lava flow from two volcanoes, Eke Crater and Haleakala Crater, formed

  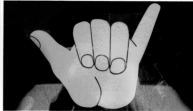

the connecting land that gives Maui the nickname of The Valley Isle. Beginning on the north shore of this valley, the famous Road to Hana gently hugs the coastline for over 50 miles and 600 plus curves as it leads the enlightened traveler on a journey of discovery. Some rush through the celebrated trip in 2-3 hours, behaving as if they were on the Los Angeles Freeway. Others learn to leisurely coax Hana's secrets out of her. As the narrow road twists and turns its' way past romantic waterfalls, lush valleys, bamboo forests, and secluded beaches of all different colors, visitors begin to experience the true Hawaii of yesteryear. In the year 2000, the Road to Hana was honored by the White House and designated as one of the United States' Millennium Legacy Trails.

A light rain may have just sprinkled the coast, blessing the land and its tropical flora and fauna. With some areas on this coast receiving over 300 inches of rain per year, dreamlike rainbows often materialize. As you drive above the stunningly blue Pacific, you'll hear the songs of native birds and smell the sweet scent of mangos, plumerias, strawberry guavas, and eucalyptus. In such a state of Zen-like perfection, you are encouraged to drive slowly and stop often to take in the natural beauty. No such thing as road rage out here in Paradise. Be sure to practice the spirit of Aloha and let faster cars go around you. Oftentimes you'll receive an appreciative kama'aina's shaka sign of greeting and thanks.

MILLENNIUM
LEGACY
TRAIL
HANA HIGHW

Give us the Road to Hana any day. They can have Highway 1, Route 66, or even the Autobahn. We're stopping to smell the roses. Or in this case, taking the time to appreciate the pineapples, sugarcane, orchids, anthuriums, hibiscus, papayas, gingers, heliconias, breadfruits, bananas, taro and much, much more. Your senses are introduced to new wonders at every dip and turn, and you begin to understand why the Polynesians (between 500-800 A.D.) sailed thousands of miles across the mysterious ocean to make these isolated islands their new home. The sea and the land provide plenty for those who learn and respect the old ways. Opportunities abound for a simple and peaceful existence all along the unspoiled Hana coast.

We're thankful that there are restful places like this still left in the world. Whether along the coast or deep in the rainforest, travelers will discover their own tranquil spots for personal reflection. The mana (spirit) is at its strongest here. We willingly surrender to nature's splendor and renew our faith in the world. Our batteries are recharged and our souls are revitalized. We understand now why the Road to Hana has come to symbolize a sort of modern day pilgrimage for romantics everywhere. After taking this wondrous journey, some enlightened travelers even decide to return to the islands for a lifetime. – P.S.

Kahului

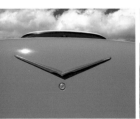

Ready, set, go! Leaving behind historical 'Iao Valley in the town of Wailuku, the Road to Hana (Route 36) officially begins in Kahului, Maui's center of commercial activity. Important business must be conducted, even here on a tropical island. Most mainland visitors arrive on Maui via Kahului Airport, but Kahului Bay is also an important gateway.

Fishermen, canoeists, and festive cruise ships share the gentle waters by the harbor. Look for the colorful kitesurfers as they soar to new heights with the help of trade winds at Kite Beach near the airport. If shopping is your sport of choice, work up a sweat at the Queen Ka'ahumanu Center, Kahului Shopping Center, Maui Mall, or the Maui Marketplace.

SHORELINE ACCESS

KITE   SURF   MAUI

Immediately after World War II, the Kahului Development Co. began building affordable new homes for local sugarcane and pineapple workers. Spurred on by the enthusiasm for this "Dream City", Kahului today maintains the largest population on the island. The renowned Maui Arts & Cultural Center

serves citizens and visitors alike by bringing the world's best entertainment to the Valley Isle. Another favorite pastime for locals is the Saturday morning Maui Swap Meet. You're bound to run into someone you know there and every item under the sun is available to shoppers at reasonable prices.

Pa'ia

With the 10,000 foot Haleakala volcano (The House of the Sun) serving as a constant companion, the time-warp begins as you enter the free-spirited town of Pa'ia. You immediately notice surfboards on the backs of trucks and colorful signs on the weather-beaten shops. Surfers, hippies, and the spiritually

inclined coexist peacefully with the day-trippers who stop here for refreshments and souvenirs. Pa'ia town also offers travelers a last chance to buy gas before heading back onto the Road to Hana. It's a long drive ahead, so play it safe and fill 'er up!

H.A. Baldwin Beach Park is a local favorite that draws bodysurfers from all over the island. Picnic areas and lifeguards provide a fun family atmosphere at this long sandy beach. Nearby, the Pa'ia Mantokuji Mission offers a quiet venue for personal reflection. Listen for the peaceful sounds of the Mission's bronze bell as it is ceremoniously rung at both sunrise and sunset.

AND ON THE SEVENTH DAY
GOD WENT SURFING

Pa'ia is an old plantation town created in 1880 when the Alexander and Baldwin Co. built its first sugar mill here. At one time, camps above the town housed 10,000 workers. A short drive up Baldwin Ave. will bring you face-to-face with remnants of the original mill. A little further on is the Father Damien Memorial at the New Holy Rosary Church.

Father Damien de Veuster (1840-1889), a Belgian priest, dedicated his life to serving those people afflicted with leprosy (aka Hansen's disease) in Hawai'i. In the 1860s, a merciless act banished those with the disease to the lonely north shore of the island of Moloka'i. Father Damien patiently worked with his care for 16 years before dying of the disease himself. His extraordinary sacrifice moves us to this very day.

Ku'au

Back now on the Road to Hana, you begin to pass the small bay and seaside community of Ku'au. Mama's Fish House, a local institution, has been serving up seafood specials in Ku'au since 1973. The restaurant's Hawaiian décor and beachfront location make it the site of many a romantic marriage proposal.

Down the road, Hoʻokipa Beach Park is rightfully called the Windsurfing Capital of the World. Hoʻokipa means hospitality, and the water enthusiasts couldn't agree more. International competitions such as the Aloha Classic are held at this beach throughout the year. Park your car on the overlook and watch the daredevil surfers and windsurfers literally fly across the waves.

Thanks to the efforts of watermen like Oʻahu's famous Duke Kahanamoku
– Father of Modern Surfing, the ancient Polynesian pastime became a full-
blown lifestyle in the first decades of the 20th century. Surfing took off on
the island of Maui also and this well known surf spot was first immortalized
in the song "Hoʻokipa Paka" by Alice Johnson in 1937.

Ha'iku & Pa'uwela

The rural areas of Ha'iku and Pa'uwela are known for their once thriving pineapple plantation villages. Beginning in the 1850's, companies such as the Ha'iku Sugar Company were instrumental in attracting pineapple planters and processors to the region. Today, small communities promoting graceful country living have sprouted alongside the productive farmland. Hidden nearby in private pineapple fields is an overlook to the world-famous big wave

break known as Peʻahi. About twelve times a year, when the conditions are just right, courageous surfers plunge into and ride the gigantic waves. Nick-named "Jaws", the oversized swells are definitely not for the faint of heart. Drive left down Hahana Street and please be respectful of the fields owned by Maui Land & Pineapple Company. For a more down-to-earth adventure, seek out an early morning cup of coffee at one of the local historic canneries.

Make note that the Hana Highway is renumbered to Route 360 near mile 16, even though you are still driving on the same scenic road. As you approach new mile marker 2, look for the many cars parked by the bridge that crosses the Hoʻolawanui Stream. You have reached the site of Twin Falls, the first of many magical waterfalls you will encounter on your excursion. This area is very popular because of its location and offers hiking trails, accessible pools, and wonderful waterfalls.

Huelo

Driving by mile marker 4, look for a colorful arrangement of mailboxes on a tight turn. Just down the country road to your left is the peaceful and remote community of Huelo. The surrounding north shore views are gorgeously serene and local bed-and-breakfasts cater to those in the know.

Huelo is home to the historic Kaulanapueo Church. Built in 1853, this pictur-esque church is named after the Hawaiian owl, a sacred bird in local legends. It is considered good luck to encounter the Pueo as these birds are said to protect individuals from harm.

Waikamoi Ridge

Driving carefully on the winding road, you have been traveling along the edge of the Koʻolau Forest Reserve for a few miles now. The colors and scents of the tropics create a lasting impression. You soon drive into the inconspicuous town of Kailua, where the field headquarters for the East Maui Irrigation Company is located. Miles and miles of tunnels and ditches deliver water

from mighty Haleakala to other parts of the island. After driving past a gentle bamboo forest, you are rewarded near mile marker 9 by Waikamoi Ridge. Follow the public trail here for spectacular scenery and a personal encounter with the best of Hawai'i's tropical flora. Waikamoi offers a wonderful and easy opportunity to stroll into a Maui rainforest.

Puohokamoa Falls

Near mile marker 11, the 30-foot Upper Puohokamoa Falls and swimming hole beckons. A short trail to the waterfall is lined with lush tropical vegetation. Hidden below the road, Lower Puohokamoa Falls secretly cascades over a 200-foot cliff. Look for other informed visitors who are parked in a small turnout just past mile marker 10 and the overview is only a few steps away.

The nearby Garden of Eden Arboretum & Botanical Garden, with 26 acres of trails, is definitely worth visiting to learn more about native Polynesian plants in an island setting. The Garden's goal is to help restore natural ecosystems and promote Hawaii's native and indigenous species. Tiny little Haipua'ena Falls is just beyond the Garden and offers a fine pool to swim and play in.

OVERLOOK

100 YEAR OLD MANGO TREE

Kaumahina &
Honomanu

Around mile marker 12, Kaumahina State Wayside Park is a great location to park your car and take in the brilliant green scenery. Picnic and camping facilities, along with several loop trails, are available at this 8-acre rest stop. Keʻanae Peninsula and the rugged coastline ahead unfolds in front of you from this spectacular vantage point.

Back on Hana Highway, look for pullouts to park in as the road swoops to unprecedented heights near Honomanu Bay. The jaw dropping panoramic views are astounding. Translated as the Bay of Sharks, the undeveloped beach park near mile marker 14 is a hit with local surfers and fishermen. We met the boys below as they released a baby hammerhead shark back into the ocean.

Keʻanae

Around mile marker 15, a wonderful botanical garden with a mile-long nature hike awaits you at the Keʻanae Arboretum. Tropical trees and taro are cultivated here right next to the gently flowing Piʻinaʻau Stream. Just a little further down the road is the village of Keʻanae, which sits picturesquely on a

field of black lava. A tsunami siren at the scenic overlook serves as a reminder of the deadly April 1, 1946 tidal wave that struck villages all along the coast from Sprecklesville to Hana. Only the church remained standing on Keʻanae after the tsunami pounded the peninsula on that terrifying April Fool's Day.

We recommend you get to Keʻanae early to sample a hot loaf of banana bread from the Keʻanae Landing Fruit Stand. After tasting this amazing homemade treat, take your time exploring Keʻanae. Today, this area is populated mostly by Hawaiians who respectfully grow taro, work the land, and catch fish much as their ancestors once did. They are grateful for nature's generosity.

The Keʻanae Congregational Church, built in 1860, is a wonderful place to stop and contemplate the peaceful surroundings. Nearby, Blue Sapphire Pools (also known as Ching's Pond) is a popular neighborhood spot for the kids to cool off. After a dip, look for the Halfway to Hana sign and treat yourself to a Hawaiian shave ice at the local food stand there.

Wailua

Near mile marker 18 is Wailua, a quaint town famous for producing the taro that is a staple of the Hawaiian diet. Visitors usually taste poi (a purple paste made from taro) for the first time when they attend a festive luau. Look for a beautiful view of Waikani Falls across from the open fields of taro.

St. Gabriel's Church and the Coral Miracle Church are the centerpieces of idyllic Wailua. A local legend is often told to visitors about the large storm that miraculously deposited enough coral from the ocean onto Wailua Beach for completion of the aptly named Coral Miracle Church in 1860.

Near mile marker 20, Upper Waikani Falls (also known as Three Bears Falls) is one of the most popular waterfalls on Hana Highway. Depending on recent rain levels, the flow of water from this triple waterfall may be putting on quite a dazzling show for you as you drive by. Please be careful if you choose to take the short path by the bridge for a closer view of the falls.

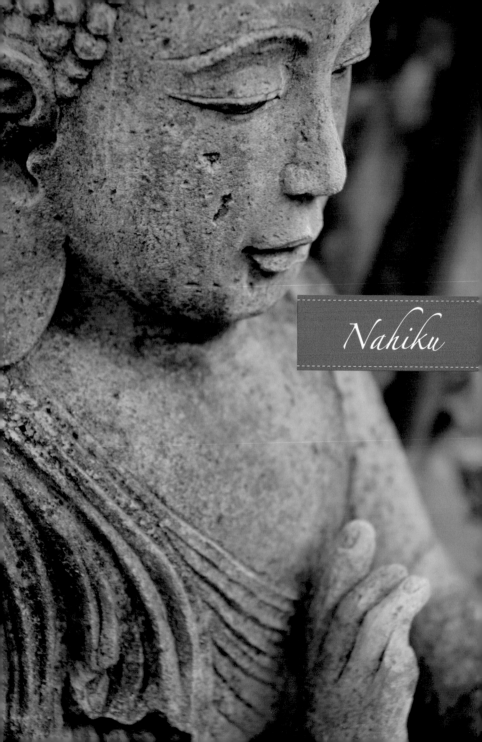

Nahiku

Pua'a Ka'a (Rolling Pig) State Park offers picnic grounds and a convenient rest area just past mile marker 22. Walk the short path from the parking lot to explore the accessible waterfalls and swimming holes. After drying off, take the winding road east again as you begin making your way to the old seaside community of Nahiku.

Hanawi Falls offers another wonderful photo opportunity just past mile marker 24. The Hanawi Stream is spring-fed so more than one waterfall can usually be seen here. A mile further, just past mile marker 25, is tiny Makapipi Falls. Look over the bridge railing on Hana Highway to see the trickling stream fall into a perfect blue pool.

Immediately after the bridge, turn left down a winding 3-mile road to reach the once bustling village of Nahiku. At the turn of the century, companies such as the Nahiku Rubber Company planted rubber trees in anticipation of the growing needs of the automobile industry. The heavy rain on this section of the coast however, ruined the fledgling enterprises.

Before the road was built, coastal steamers once docked regularly at the village wharf to deliver passengers and goods. Today, Nahiku is often noted for some of the village's wealthy property owners. The Nahiku Coffee Shop and Smoked Fish Stand is a great stop for refreshments. Also, local fruit and flower stands from this point on offers fresh items for sale on the honor system.

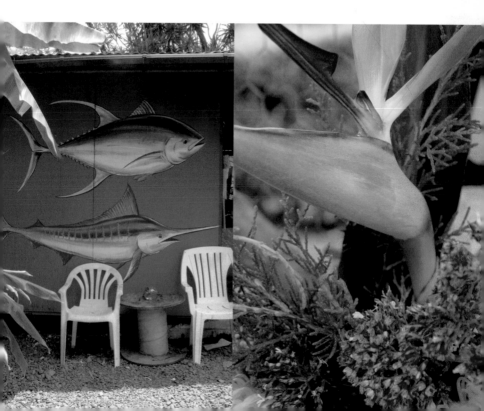

Wai'anapanapa

Ulaʻino Road at mile marker 32 will lead you to Piʻilanihale Heʻiau, the largest preserved ancient Hawaiian temple in the islands. This place of worship
is named after Piʻilani, a 15th century chief who wisely united the districts
of Maui. Declared a National Historic Landmark in 1966, this revered site

is located within the 472 acres of the wonderful Kahanu Garden (operated by the National Tropical Botanical Garden). Further down Ulaʻino Road is beautiful Blue Pool and its 100-foot waterfall. The sparkling falls are just a stone's throw away from the ocean's edge.

Ka'eleku Caverns' lava tube system, Honokalani Black Sand Beach, and the 3-mile long Coastal Trail are other attractions in the Wai'anapanapa (Glistening Water) State Park area. There is said to be a pool at Wai'anapanapa that inexplicably turns red once a year. Scientists claim that red-colored shrimp in the water create this annual spectacle. Hawaiian legend however, tells the sad tale of Chief Kakae and his wife Popoalaea. Kakae was an unreasonably

jealous man who became convinced that his wife had been unfaithful to him. Afraid of her husband's temper, Popoalaea hid in a cave, coming out only at night to gather food. Kakae inadvertently discovered Popoalaea's hiding place one day by spotting her reflection in the water. Enraged, he entered the cave and murdered the one person who truly loved him. The periodic blood-red water at Waiʻanapanapa serves as a reminder of this terrible tragedy.

Hana

Paradise! As you drive into the small coastal town of Hana around mile marker 33, you comprehend why the Hawaiian chiefs fought for centuries to lay claim to this most special of places. Time seems to have stood still on this part of the coast as the friendly people live a simple and perhaps more meaningful life than ours. There are no strip-malls or fast food chain restaurants here. Take some time to quietly savor the details.

 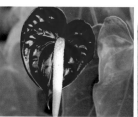 

Several places of worship including St. Mary's Catholic Church, Wananalua Congregational Church and Hana Hongwanji Buddhist Temple await visitors with open arms. The landscape, with cattle and horses grazing in the pasture, is peaceful and breathtaking. In 1979, George Harrison of the Beatles immortalized the town with his song "Soft-Hearted Hana". The famous musician fell in love with the Hana region and lived in nearby Nahiku.

When the coastal road first opened in 1926, Hana celebrated with a luau lasting for two days. Even though the road made driving to central Maui possible, it was nothing more than a muddy path for many years. Stories abound of total strangers exchanging cars going in opposite directions when a mudslide suddenly stopped their forward progress. The Hana Cultural Center & Museum is a wonderful place to learn more about the colorful local history.

At Hana Beach, there is a plaque marking Queen Kaʻahumanu's birthplace on Kaʻuiki Hill. Kaʻahumanu was the favorite wife of King Kamehameha I, who united the island kingdom in 1810. Legend also tells of Kaʻuiki, a young man who fell in love with Noenoe, daughter to the demigod Maui. To keep their love eternal, Maui used his magical powers to turn Kaʻuiki into the landmark hill and Noenoe into the light rain that comes to embrace him daily.

Some of the most beautiful and spectacular scenery in Hana can be found at several local beaches. Koki Beach has a stunning view of 'Alau Island, the site where legendary Maui first pulled the Hawaiian Islands out of the sea. Wonderful Hamoa Beach is located just around the corner from Koki. The writer James Michener, famous for his novel on Hawaii, raved about the "perfectly

formed" Hamoa Beach. Well-hidden Kaihalulu (Roaring Sea) Beach, located in a gorgeous cove, was formed by volcanic cinders and is shockingly red in color. Former First Lady Hillary Clinton, on a trip to Hana with her mother, hiked the precipitous trail into this secret and isolated attraction. Look for the trailhead near the Community Center at the end of Ua Kea Road in town.

HASEGAWA
GENERAL STORE

The Hasegawa General Store, established in 1910, is a fourth-generation family store made famous in 1961 by Paul Weston's catchy song of the same name. Think of any item you may need, from sunburn creams to a ukulele, and it is probably sitting on one of Hasegawa's well-stocked shelves. The store's slogan is "Far from Waikiki" and that's just the way the Hana locals prefer it.

In 1849, George Wilfong started the first sugar plantation on this part of the coast and many other operations soon followed. Sugar was king here until World War II, when C. Brewer & Co. decided to close down the largest plantation in Hana. Paul Fagan, an entrepreneur from San Francisco, stepped in to create new opportunities for the town. Sensing that sugar would not provide security for the future generations of Hana, Fagan purchased 14,000 acres of land and shipped in cattle to create The Hana Ranch in 1944.

Believing in the potential of tourism, Paul Fagan and his wife Helene also established an inn in 1946 for luxury travelers that would later be known as the Hotel Hana-Maui. This AAA Four Diamond resort continues to impress today as the perfect location for honeymoons and romantic getaways. The Hotel offers wonderful activities such as horseback riding and private Jeep tours. The on-site Honua Spa and the Hana Coast Gallery also add to the first-class ambience. Go ahead and pamper yourself!

Hotel HANA·MAUI

HOTEL *Hana-Maui*

HAWAIIAN ISLANDS

HOTEL *Hana-Maui*
HAWAIIAN ISLANDS

Hotel **HANA-MAUI**

HOTEL *Hana-Maui*
HAWAIIAN ISLANDS

HOTEL *Hana-Maui*
HAWAIIAN ISLANDS

As a part-owner of the San Francisco Seals baseball team of the Pacific Coast League, Fagan even flew in the players and a group of mainland sportswriters to Hana for a spring training publicity tour. It was one of those newspaper writers who coined the catchy nickname "Heavenly Hana" to describe this remote tropical paradise.

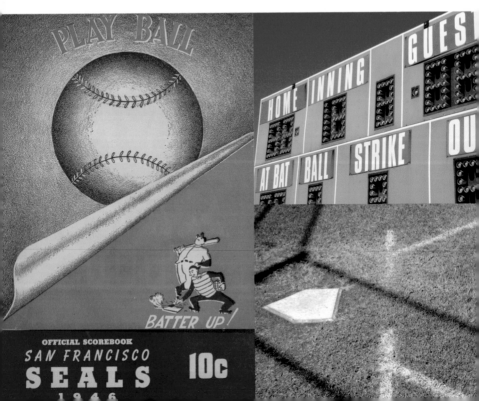

Partially because of Fagan's vision, this small coastal town continued to thrive. Today, many of the local citizens work for Hana Ranch and the Hotel Hana-Maui. For a panoramic view that will remain with you for a lifetime, hike up Lyons Hill to visit Fagan's Memorial, a lava cross erected in appreciation of Paul Fagan and his generosity.

Kipahulu

Beyond the town of Hana, the road (renumbered Hwy. 31) begins to twist and curve its way through the tropical rainforest of Kipahulu Valley. Well-hidden Waioka (Venus) Pool, located at mile marker 48, is a naturally formed pool found in an incredible oceanfront setting. 95-foot Wailua Falls, at mile marker 45, is one of Maui's most photographed attractions. Newlyweds love to use popular Wailua as a backdrop for that perfect honeymoon portrait.

Ten miles after Hana, visitors swim in a series of pools at 'Ohe'o Gulch (part of Haleakala National Park), blissfully unaware that new species of flora and fauna are still being discovered in the wilderness directly above them. Promoted as the Seven Sacred Pools by a publicist, there are actually more than two dozen pools to swim and play in. For a real workout, hike the 4-mile roundtrip Pipiwai Trail, which follows the Pipiwai Stream through a bamboo forest, to experience 200-foot Makahiku Falls, and 400-foot Waimoku Falls.

Over the years, many celebrities and the well-to-do have come to call this area their home. In relative anonymity, they have worked to responsibly preserve the beauty and accessibility of the land. We thank them for their gracious efforts in sharing Kipahulu with us. Charles Lindbergh, the famous aviator, lived here for a time and was buried at the local Palapala Hoʻomau Congregational Church in 1974. Stricken with cancer and adamantly wanting to fly

home to Maui, Lindbergh told his doctor, "I'd rather spend two days alive on Maui than two months alive in this hospital here in New York City." Although difficult to find, visitors today can pay their respects to the "Lone Eagle" at the simple limestone coral church. On Lindbergh's dignified headstone are two lines from Psalms 139: "…If I take the wings of the morning, and dwell in the uttermost parts of the sea…"

Leaving Kipahulu, the unpaved road leads past spectacular panoramas to arrive at the ranching and fishing community of Kaupo Village. Fewer than 30 full-time residents continue to live in this magnificent outpost. The beautiful and isolated Hui'aloha Church, built in 1857, sits alone facing the open seas with small Mokulau Beach fronting the dramatic shoreline.

Peacefulness and tranquility surround you on this last leg of your road trip.
Give yourself plenty of time to take it all in. While driving back towards
"civilization" on the bumpy road, stop off at the historic Kaupo Store for
some refreshments and conversation. Built in 1925, the colorful store exudes a
timeless quality with its wonderful display of antiques, bottles and cameras.

In many ways, the Road to Hana teaches us to take the time each day to discover life's simple joys and pleasures. Life isn't merely about speeding towards yet another task or destination. Those funny bumper stickers that read "Slow Down – This Ain't The Mainland" are absolutely right. At the completion of this wonderful journey, most people will tell you that they have been changed forever. It is an encouraging sign in today's cynical world. That is the power of the Road to Hana, Maui. Aloha and thank you for traveling with us.

Aloha

Credits:

All photographs by Anna Tan and Pak So with the exception of the images and photographers credited herein. A big mahalo especially to Ki So, our special contributing photographer, for flying to Maui and taking the journey with us. You are a consummate professional!

All vintage photographic images and illustrations are from the collection of Pak So and credit is given where the artist is known. Many vintage images are from early photographs or postcards where the artist remains unidentified. Any credit omissions are unintentional and will be corrected in future printings.

Photographic images by Ki So,
Shadow of palm tree, 4; Children on beach, 6; Lava flow drinks, 27; Ku'au Cove, 28; Yard and surfboards, 35; Fence, 36; Twin Falls, 37; Twin Falls, 38; Kaulanapueo Church, 42; Jeep on road, 56; Falls at Pua'a Ka'a State Park, 76; Makapipi Falls, 77; Blue Pool, 82; Blue Pool, 86; Honokalani Black Sand Beach, 88; Hana town from Lyon's Hill, 90; Trees in Hana town, 92; St. Mary's Catholic Church, 93; Two cows, 97; Cows on hill, 97; Kaihalulu Beach, 102; 'Ohe'o Gulch, 120; Waimoku Falls, 123; sunset, 125; Road in Kaupo, 128

Photographic images by Ray Jerome Baker:
Haleakala volcano, 20; Surfer, 57; Girl with ukulele, 58

Photographic image by Billy Howell:
Boy drinking from coconut, 44; Island girl with flowers, 89

Illustrations by John Kelly:
Bread Fruit, 41; Lei Maker, 99

Illustrations by Frank MacIntosh:
Hula girls, 26

Photographic image by Dave Martin:
Island girl with lei, 115

Illustrations by Ted Mundorff:
Red Hibiscus, 44; Torch Ginger, 45

Photographic images by Mike Roberts:
Island girl by waterfall, 1; Hawaiian Airlines Super Convair, 10; Lei seller and cruise ship, 11; Lei stringer, 66, Lei stringer, 74; Luau, 98; Hotel Hana-Maui menus, 105, 107-109

Photographic image by Hobron Smith:
Island girl with orchids, 49

Photographic image by Werner Stoy:
Bird of Paradise, 70

Photographic image by Manuel Tan Jr.:
Hana Highway above Honomanu Bay, 56

Photographic image by Underwood:
Charles Lindbergh, 124

Photographic image by J.J. Williams:
Tasting poi, 65

About the Authors:

On a beautiful day in May, the authors Anna Tan and Pak So were married on the peaceful Hana coast of Maui, Hawaii. *Paradise: Road to Hana, Maui* is their loving tribute to one of the world's most spectacular and romantic island destinations. Anna and Pak continue to share the spirit of aloha through their distinctive gift and publishing company, Hana In May (www.HanaInMay.com).

Anna Tan (www.annatan.com) is an award-winning art director who creates eye-catching graphic design work for clients in the publishing, arts, and corporate industries. Her work has been recognized in the field with awards from Graphis, Black Book AR100, and The Society of Publication Design. You can't design a better sunset than the ones in Hawaii and Anna loves watching the technicolor skies from her personal stretch of sand at Kamaole Beach Park in Kihei, Maui.

Pak So (www.pakso.com) is a painter, writer and passionate collector of vintage travel images. He is actively involved in the arts and has worked to organize collections and exhibitions for prestigious Christie's Auction House, Pace/MacGill Gallery, and the Howard Greenberg Gallery in New York. Pak loves going off the beaten path to sample artful local dishes and swears by the tempura udon at Ichiban Okazuya in Wailuku, Maui.

Tell us your tales of romance and discovery in Hawaiʻi.
We would love to share some wonderful stories on our website.
Please visit us at www.HanaInMay.com.

Aloha!